# Of The First Magnitude

## ~I~

# Copyright Notice:

Read it!

Integrate it!

Live it!

*Truth*, that is...

Emergent Strategies LLC
PO Box 245
Winona, MO. 65588
https://3m3r3g.com
orders@3m3rg3.com

Ordering Information:

ISBN: 978-1-7337454-2-0

Quantity sales. Special discounts are available on quantity purchases by corporations, associations, and others. For details, contact the publisher at the address above.

**Cover Art**: Sam Whelan - https://www.samwhelan.net/

# ~ Volume 3 ~

# Quantum Engineering

## Introspecting the Rabbit Hole

By Michael Phoenix

# Table of Contents

# Intro

## Read This If You Are Reading This!

Inside these words is a sight *into* life, *see* it, *feel* it, and you will know freedom. *Proceeding forward from this moment with an* **open mind** *is beneficial to Seeing. Proceeding forward from this moment with an* **open heart** *is beneficial to Feeling.* Proceed as **YOU** *will.*

Verse 1: $E=mc^2$

Verse 2: Theory of Relativity: Special and General

Verse 3: Uncertainty Principle

Verse 4: Wave/Particle Duality

Verse 5: Quantum Entanglement

Verse 6: Quantum Field Theory

Verse 7: Quantum Electrodynamics

<u>If</u> you are of an empirical mind, one that *sees* these fundamental principles as basic laws, <u>then</u> you may be closer to home than you think.

Moving through the doors of your **heart** to *offer* them as the *guiding principles* **in Your *living* of Life**, and *trust* that your heart will do the rest — have faith — And you will be home…

<u>If</u> and <u>when</u> you allow your heart to be the *guide* in life, you will <u>then</u> *feel* Life.

You have a choice to exist *in the suffering* of life for *an eternity of hell's sacrifice*…

And, you have a choice to exist *in the joy* of life for *an infinitude of heaven's light*…

Because ultimately, in the movement, "<u>It</u>" *is* all **One —** absolutely!

**You *Feel* what YOU believe!**

<u>If</u> you are one of the heart who moves *in* faith, <u>then</u> you are already home, you simply must *see* it in all-that-is as the function of reality.

Moving through the veil of your **mind** to *operate* as a *functional unit* of quantized expression **in Your *living* of Life**, and *see* the light extending Life *into* all that you see.

<u>If</u> and <u>when</u> you allow your sight to be light in life, you will <u>then</u> *see* Life.

You have a choice to exist *in the suffering* of life for *an eternity of hell's sacrifice…*

And, you have a choice to exist *in the joy* of life for *an infinitude of heaven's light…*

Because ultimately, in the movement, "<u>It</u>" *is* all **One –** absolutely!

**You *See* what YOU believe!**

**WARNING!** This is **<u>NOT</u>** a scientific thesis; this is merely a musing of philosophical **_inquiry_** contextualized by scientific concepts – a pondering of certain guiding *dynamics* that have been discovered regarding Nature **AND the application** of those dynamics to *Life* as an <u>*experience*</u>. A contemplation of the idea that humans are existent quantum derivative objects that have influence in the fabric of space and time, more commonly referred to as "reality".

What we know we don't know can be quantified by the percentage of 96%. Saying this another way, that which can be directly observed, quantified with specific measurements, and subsequently characterized with certain qualities represents only 4% of the universe as we know it to exist. The remaining 96% is only known only by its influence on that which we can identify. And **indirect** identification.

In other words, the vast majority of "reality" is unknown to our rational minds. Furthermore, it cannot be known by a mind state that subjects itself to only considering a rationale "needing to see to believe". The rational aspect of the mind in this reality is composed of the stuff of the universe. Using the "stuff" of this universe in attempt to peer beyond the "stuff" is an uphill battle. *Knowing* That-Which exists beyond the manifolds of physical reality requires moving into a paradigm that views reality from a perspective that is 'meta' to the physical. An Empire of Rational Knowledge[1].

---

[1] For more on the Empire of Rational Knowledge, read iRise: An Algorhythm of Freedom; Article 1, Chapter 2 -- "Epistemological Axiom"

The manifold confines of holomorphic fields enveloping the physical densities of reality keeps our "knowing" imprisoned to a context of ~*this*~ point-of-view. Keeping this in-mind as you contemplate that-which influences your current paradigm is critical. *You know less than you think you know.* Accepting this fact of reality **requires** humility. **Unwavering pride** in your intellectual understanding is a trap of your own making. Learn to open your awareness to that which you cannot perceive with your physical constructs. Considering this as possible is the first step.

Proceed if you so *choose*...

# V<sub>erse</sub> 1

## E=mc2

**"E"** is defined as energy - the *capacity* of a system <u>to do work</u>.

**"="** is defined as *equals* - to be *equal* to something else; equal - evenly *balanced* between opposite sides.

**"m"** is defined as **mass** - the property of an **object** that is a **measure** of its inertia, the amount of **matter** it contains, and its *influence* in a gravitational **field**, wherein matter is defined as the **material substance** of the universe that has mass, **occupies space**, and is *convertible to energy*.

**"multiplied by"** is defined as *multiplication* - the *act of* multiplying, or *the condition of being* multiplied, an aggregation of groups.

**"c"** is defined as the-speed-of-light (in a vacuum) - 299,792,458 meters per second.

**"2"** is defined as squared - the product resulting from multiplying a number or term by itself.

---

Here's a question for you… have you ever visualized light traveling at 300 million meters per second? First visualize 300 million meters (Here's a tip: 300 million meters is roughly 186,000 miles. The moon is about 238,000 miles from the earth). Then square that visualization ($3.4596 \times 10^{10}$). Then multiply that times an object's mass. If you have been able to do that, then you've visualized how much "energy" there is in an object's physical existence… off the charts? Another way to ask that, can you even conceptualize that amount of energy as an image in your mind?

If all energy is conserved, and it merely "transitions" between "states" of energy and "forms" of matter (huh… that's interesting, this description "energy conservation" sounds *frighteningly* similar to the concept of "spirit" and its relationship to a "soul"… but that's besides the point), what happens to the information that is "stored" *in* the energy *as* the energy? Does the information stay the same or does it change with every transition? Does the entropy upon conversion ambiguate the information in the energy?

Sure the "state" of the atom changes, but what about that "stuff" that makes up the atoms?

What about the *energy*, the energy that is said to be there yet is unverifiable because there is no direct way to test the actual energy itself? What's the deal with this "mystical" energy anyway - what *is* energy?

Without energy, there is no movement. All mass is in motion. All mass is inextricably linked to *energy*. For an entity to have **mass** IN the physical universe, it must be composed of matter, and matter is the *compiling* substance of the entire universe. Therefore, **all matter** has an *inherent energy*. It's quite redundant.

What *is* <u>energy</u>? The "ability *to do work*." In other words, "we have no knowledge of what energy is."[2]

Through observation and experimentation, energy can only be qualitatively examined and quantified accordingly. From the context of limited sight, it is only *seen* what energy *does*. That *seeing* is limited to the perspective it was observed from.

Ahhhh subjectivity...

According to the *law* of the *conservation of energy*, through the assorted transitions that **matter** *processes* through within space-time, the **quantity** of *energy* stays the same. Within a closed system, and with a single observer, relativity becomes the dominant perspective of energy that is qualitatively quantified and quantitatively qualified.

Within that *relative* matrix of observation, mass and energy can be *seen* as two **quantifiable** aspects of the same qualitative unit; thus, $E=mc^2$. *Energy* (the quality) equals *mass* and *the speed of light*

---

[2] Richard Feynman, *Six Easy Pieces*, pg. 71

*squared* (the quantities). Qualitative quantification. Quantified qualifications.

Energy can thusly be identified as an ***expression*** of a *unit* of an existentiality. And mass can also be identified as an ***expression*** of that same **unit**.

In the observable world, there exists a universe composed of matter which is more fundamentally defined as a mass/energy coupling. This coupling can be identified as the **emergence** of the underlying unit that gives rise to the quantifiable nature of that which is *observed*. And *through observation* the *qualities* are recognized – **identification**.

Ahhhh objectivity…

If, in the observable world, entities exist (existentiality) with quantifiable mass/energy ratios, such as humans, that are expressions of the same Unit or Entity that exists as the foundation of all matter, what then is ***that*** Unit or *Entity* ***which*** gives rise to the effulging of localized sentient observables that the observer observes within the observable world?

Presuppositions inherent to existentiality are evidenced by such existentialities. Existence exists; identification evidences this. Awareness exists; experience evidences this. Awareness of existence is always happening; identifying one's experience evidences this. And its all *energy* in some *form* or *another*.

In a *relative* <u>sense</u>, it can only be known what energy *does*. Relative observation is *dependent upon the localizable framework* and **structure** that existing as an *interacting matrix* of energy in all its various **forms**.

**Me** as an *observer* and the world **I** *perceive* is a localized quantifiable mass/energy ratio of the same underlying Unit providing existentiality to all of existence. A point that moves, i.e. **Me,** or singularity of action in a matrix. All *sensing* of that localization is the beginning of identification of it. Identification occurs with recognition of what-is.

Even the finest teaching is not the Tao itself.

Even the finest name is insufficient to define it.

Without words, the Tao can be experienced,

and without a name, it can be known.[3]

---

[3] Tao Te Ching, Verse 1, translation by Stan Rosenthal.

# Segue 1

Imagine it's a pitch-black night. Hidden behind a thick cloud cover are the stars and the moon. The only light visible is your flashlight. All that you can see is that which is in the *visible* ray of light.

You focus your attention and awareness out as far as you can to see what's out there. You notice it's difficult. Things tend to be "more hidden" in the camouflage of darkness.

You know there are more things *out there*. But you just can't see them. You start to move your light around *to get a better perspective* of the situation. Even then, you can't see that which is *beyond the horizon* of night.

The next night, you go outside and you notice the stars in the sky, so you go to your telescope to see out into space. You look as far as you can, and all you can see is as far as your telescope will allow. That which it magnifies to be visible to the naked eye.

You see beautiful things – planets, stars, asteroids, galaxies, galaxy clusters – all that *and* more. Yet, all you can see is as far as the light that's visible to your **perception** *through* the telescope.

The next night, you go to the Hubble Telescope. You look at the images coming back from that, AND, you find that you see waaaaaaaaaaaay out into space. Yet, as far as you can see is as far as the light is visible to your **perception**, again, *through* the telescope.

Once more, you report back beautiful things - novas, supernovas, quasars, pulsars – all that plus additional phenomena.

Yet again, all you can see is as far as the light is visible to *your* perception through the telescope.

So what's really "out there?"

What's out there when you're outside at night and all you can see is what's *in the light?*

What's out there when you're looking through the telescope at the beautiful phenomena out in deep space?

And, what does "out there" refer to with regards to *your* perception of "out there?"

Let him who seeks continue seeking until he
finds. When he finds, he will become troubled.
When he becomes troubled, he will be
astonished, and he will rule of the All.[4]

---

[4] Gospel of Thomas, verse 2. Translation by Lambdin, Grenfell & Hunt.

# V<sub>erse</sub> 2

## Theory of Relativity: Special & General

**Special:**

1.  Every piece of matter within the fabric of space-and-time has a *frame of reference* according to the position at which the matter is located.

2.  *All observation within the universe is relative* to the object's (piece of matter's) frame of reference.

3.  $E=mc^2$.

4.  particle/wave *Duality* of Light.

5.  et al.

**General:**

1.  Space and time becomes *warped* with the presence of matter

2.  The fabric of the universe is composed of 3 dimensions of space and 1 dimension of time - a space-time continuum – *space-time*.

3.  et al.

—

Why must it be called a space-time *continuum*? Why is the *label* on this *concept* a "continuum" – "a link between two things, or a continuous series of things, that blend into each other so gradually and seamlessly that it is impossible to say where one becomes the next?"[5]

Is it possible that "it" is in fact *one* unified *whole* – a unity that *transitions* from state to state at localized reference points within a dynamic fabric composed of space and time? A multi-manifold fabric that is directly influenced by the energy and momentum of the matter and radiation that is present?

Allow the mind to contemplate the rhetorical nature of this question. Notice if there is an immediate and direct answer offered by the mind; especially if there is no evidence that supports the answer. Direct answers without evidence often serve ignorance rather than knowledge.

Might not the entities existing within the context of the continuum be "reference points" within the *frame* of the continuum, a *reference point* that is itself a multi-manifold entity?

Contemplate…

All *action* that occurs within the context of the "fabric" of space-time is dependent upon the relative nature of the fabric. There

---

[5] Definition of continuum: Encarta Dictionary; English (North America).

is no absolute position *within* "space-time" that supersedes any other position. *All points of reference <u>within</u> the context of the fabric are each relative to the point of reference,* <u>none more dominant than the next.</u>

Perhaps there reference points that are more kinetic in its process of energy momentum. And some reference points may be more expressive than other reference points. Coalescing, moving, and radiating vast quantities of quantum potential into cosmic kinesthetics.

*All* observation occurring within ~**this**~ context is *relative to the position from which the observation was observed.* There is no way to absolutely determine "what *is*" from within a framework that has no absolute position with which to base judgment of "what *is*."

**All** absolute judgment is subsequently baseless. There is no absolute foundation to determine the judgment. All judgment within the context of *the fabric* is relative – relative to the position from which the *judgment* was determined.

The object is a subject. The subject is an object.

Judgments determined from within the context of the fabric are relative, and as such, they possess no more *ultimate* validity than any other *relative judgment.*

All entities composed within the context of the "fabric" of space-time will consequently be subjected to the relative nature of the fabric – 3 dimensions of space and 1 of time.

*All observations* of *any entity* within the fabric will also be subject to the relative nature of the fabric - 3 dimensions of space and 1 of time.

An entity's space-time "frame of reference" is composed of, the "observation" of all relative *inter-action* occurring within the fabric of space-time. The actual "frame" from which all "reference" emanates is relative to the location where AND how the *observation* takes place.

In perceiving the fabric, the *perceiving* through which observation takes place, the actual ability to observe anything is made possible by electromagnetic radiation, a portion of which is visible light. Without a "thing" to "observe" within the fabric, there can be no *observation*.

Observing a thing depends on a continuum wherein a most basic interaction is summarized as $E=mc^2$. The energy of the whole of space-time is all its mass moving. Without movement, there is no "thing" to observe in this framework. Observation is occurring continuously. The constant here is change.

The "observation" is made possible through the emission and subsequent reflection of light *from* the object that is being observed – and thus, an *inter-action* occurs, an interaction of energy with its-*self*.

Constant action and interaction of energy is the basic nature of the fabric of space-time, constantly changing *form,* from one moment to the next. And yet, it is still **all** derived from *One* Unit or Entity

The act of forgiving accepts the fact that

each perceivable *individual* exists as an *object*,

while the backdrop of space-time's relativity

supplies the *localized* platform of 'what *is*'[6]

[6] Michael Phoenix

# $S$egue 2

Try this, if you will…

Sit wherever the physical body is currently located. Imagine a path opening up before it; this path is your immediate future. Now imagine another path open up directly to the right of the body; this path is also your immediate future. Now a path to directly to the left, now a path to the rear, and straight up. Imagine all the *infinite* angles, the paths, the possibilities open around the body. All possibilities of the immediate future, and you strain to see down each path - *the veil of what is unknown.*

All these paths have a foggy mist covering each path, all paths are obscured. The future is obscure. The only thing that you can really make out is what is immediately before you, and all you see is the *opening* to the paths, and as you look down each path, all you see is a dense fog obscuring the path.

As each moment is passing, all that is lit is the opening to each path, the fog of obscurity that is the future *never* lifts. Although only the opening to each path can be seen. Each opening changes from moment to moment. With each change, the opening *appears* different… changing scenery each moment.

Consider that "time" is merely the *movement* of *observation* through one path, yet all paths exist **simultaneously** – i.e.

simultaneous time. All that can be observed within the constraint of "time" is the one path that is the moment of Now. The moment that *is*.

The *perception* of time acts as the candle illuminating the individual path *through* simultaneous time, yet all other paths exist as possibilities in the moment of Now.

Let's assume for a moment that this is the case; that all other paths exist as simultaneous possibilities. Then a question is, if all possibilities are *actual* possibilities, what is Reality?

If all possibilities exist, and *"time"* is simply a continuous *movement of* moment to moment *observation* and **decision** through *an individual path*; what then is The Reality that gives rise to, and allows for, the individual path? And for the simultaneous existence of all possibilities? What is the Reality that provides the potential and gives the possibility for **all** this to exist?

Perhaps the *One* Reality?

If all possibilities exist, perhaps it is not the path of physical action that defines one's existence, but instead the choice that leads to the path of action. Maybe it's even deeper than choice, perhaps it is the vacuum of freedom that gives rise to the possibility of having a choice?

If all paths already exist, then the *observation* of the movement of "time" comes about by defining one's self by the *choice* rather than the path, for the path can only be observed *after* the choice has been made. The choice *directs* action.

If this is the case, *what* gives rise to the possibility of *choice*?

# V<sub>erse</sub> 3

## Uncertainty Principle

**Uncertainty:** "Fact of being uncertain; the quality or state of being uncertain. Unpredictable thing; something that nobody can predict or guarantee."[7]

**Principle:** "Basic assumption; *an important underlying law or assumption required in a system of thought.* Ethical standard; a standard of moral or ethical decision-making. *Way of working; the basic way in which something works.*"[8] [emphasis added]

**Uncertainty Principle:** "a principle in quantum mechanics holding that it is impossible to determine both the current position and future momentum of a particle at the same time."[9]

—

---

[7] Encarta Dictionary: English (North America)

[8] Ibid.

[9] Ibid.

If obscurity arises from concrete determination of the *dynamic activity* of the basic nature of physical existence, what does that tell us about the essence of *dynamic activity*?

*Dynamic* presupposes a movement inasmuch as *activity* presupposes the state of being active.

And in this regard *concrete determination* refers to certainty.

Yet, according to the basic nature of physical existence, "certainty" is merely a cloud of fiction holding back the light of clarity.

The ever-changing nature of the fabric of physical existence begets the *essence of impermanence,* the lack of a **permanent** form of **things**. No-thing stays the same, and where there is a *beginning*, there is also a corresponding *end*; the *Alpha* and the *Omega*.

If *things* are uncertain, what about the certainty of this moment's existence? Not the circumstantial appearances, but the fact that this moment exists as a cosmological constant. That certainty. Where does it arise from?

So do not worry about tomorrow; for tomorrow

will care for itself. Each day has enough trouble

of its own.[10]

[10] The Gospel of Matthew, chapter 6, verse 34

# Segue 3

Here's a question for you, if the nature of physical existence is such that impermanence reigns supreme, what's the point in determining a material future that is indeterminable except in the moment of Now?

The idea you have in your imagination about what tomorrow will be cannot determine the actuality of tomorrow. Only tomorrow can determine tomorrow, and the determination will occur in the moment tomorrow becomes the choices being made today.

Speaking of these, and thinking metaphorically...

What does "tomorrow" symbolize? Future.

And what does "today" symbolize? Now.

Why ruminate on the obscurity of tomorrow when Today bears witness to *Life*? That which you worry about occurring tomorrow can only be resolved today. Living with reverence for *Life* right now opens the door of a better tomorrow.

# V<sub>erse</sub> 4

## Wave/Particle Duality

**Wave:** Oscillation of energy.

**Particle:** Object with finite mass

**Duality:** Something consisting of two parts

**Wave/Particle Duality:** Light and matter exhibit properties of both a wave and a particle.

—

So what is existence, a wave or a particle?

Would that not depend on how **I** look at it?

Could it then be considered either?

Or is it more appropriate to say that both light and matter *function* as **both** a wave **and** a particle depending upon *how* it is observed, by Me, the observer? By *what I am looking at?*

# $S$egue 4

**Part 1:**

Have you ever heard of a tribe of Beings known as the Slegna Kra? A discreet group of beings that span back since before recorded history. Shrouded in mystery are the beings of the Slegna Kra.

Would you be interested to know that this tribe lives among you, in plain sight for all to see, all over the world?

Born of many different cultures, races and nationalities, this tribe is not a tribe of birthright. It is a tribe that exists solely for the advancement of every one, and membership in this tribe is not determined by anyone but the one who seeks to belong to it.

You may very well be a member of this tribe and know it not. In fact, all people alive today have the capacity within them to be a conscious member of this tribe.

It is *not* a tribe that seeks to expand their control and dominance over others, for this goes against the very nature of their character.

There is no controlling dictator of this tribe. All members are members because they have the capacity to govern themselves according to their inmost *spirit of Life*.

There is no initiation to enter the tribe, except the initiation of choice. Many have long sought to enter into the ranks of this tribe, yet most get snared in the trap of darkness. Sitting idly in the delusion of sloth. Denouncing the blessing of *Life* that *is* gifted to them - *gifted solely for the purpose of entering into the ranks of this tribe.*

**Part 2:**

A man once stood upon a riverbank watching the water wisp away with grace and ease. As he stood there, he noticed clouds begin to crest over the peaks of the snow-capped mountains on the horizon.

Looking to his right, he could see the river fall over the edge of a waterfall, only to see it make its way out into the ocean.

As he moved his gaze back towards the waters of the river lapping its cool caress upon his ankles, he wondered about the water.

He asked the water, "What makes you what you are?" Not expecting the water to answer, he sat down to clear his mind in meditation. As he sat just out of the water, a voice softly whispered from the back of his mind, *move into the water.* Simultaneously a pulse of joy reverbed through his chest.

He could not think of a reason why not, so he gently scooted down into the water. Now immersed waist deep in the water, he began to meditate. As his mind quieted and his body relaxed, he felt as if he melted into the water itself.

The river was no longer distinct to him, for all he could *feel*, he was the water. He felt himself move across the many rocks on the bottom. He felt himself swirl in upon himself, caress the riverbank and fall over edge of the waterfall. He felt himself fall as snow over the mountaintops, stream down into the river and finally into the ocean.

Yet, all the while, he was still very much himself, distinctly *being human*, but no longer separate from the water.

Remaining united with the water, he again asked the question, "What makes you what you are?"

He again heard the voice in his mind, *is not your real question, what makes me who I am?*

"Okay," he said out loud, "What makes me who I am?" As he said this, a rush of chills ignited in the soles of his feet and shot upwards through his legs, up his spine and out the top of his head.

*I am who am. You are me, I am you,* the voice said. *Form matters not. The Great Spirit is what makes you who you are, and it is everything...there is nowhere you are not.*

# V erse 5

## Quantum Entanglement

**Quantum:** "smallest unit… used to measure a physical property"[11]

**Entanglement:** "to make something become twisted up in a mass…"[12]

**Quantum Entanglement:** "a quantum mechanical phenomenon in which the quantum states of two or more objects are linked together so that one object can no longer be adequately described without full mention of its counterpart — even though the individual objects may be spatially separated."[13]

—

---

[11] Encarta Dictionary: English (North America)

[12] Ibid

[13] Definition from: http://en.wikipedia.org/wiki/Quantum_entanglement, accessed 01-09-2009

Two objects… separated by space, somehow linked… not separated by time… what does this mean for me?

The quantum state of Me, all the quantum particles that compose Me, are "somehow linked" to objects that are separated by space. "Me" cannot be defined without mention of the counterpart objects.

Why?

Because the counterpart objects that my quantum state is entangled to must also be included in the description.

Without the yin, there can be no yang, and vice versa. Each unit is composed such that neither one is sufficient without the other. All aspects are part of the whole and the whole composes each aspect.

In the "entanglement" inherent in the substratum of my existence, I am all that I see. By the very act of observing, I become entangled with that which I observe, and I can no longer be accurately described without mention of all my observations and experiences.

It all rests entirely upon what **I** am looking at…

What I choose to see, *apparently*…

# $S$egue 5

At a moment within time, when the roaring sound of war's fatal clash echoes through the brick and mortar of planet Earth's spiritually destitute civilizations, there is but one alternative…

When snatched from the fuzzy warmth of childhood's innocence and thrust into the upheaval of juvenile pettiness, there is but one alternative…

With the countless years of Wisdom's soothing touch beckoning to be realized; quietly calling to be released from the prison of confusion, patiently She waits for her children to grow up.

She must wait for her children to awake from the slumber of their self-created nightmares. She must wait for them to recognize what they have never lost. She must wait for them to open the secret chamber of their sacredness, that they have long since closed and forgotten.

To release the indignation of adolescent righteousness, a planet of humans will some-day grow to illuminate the seeds of their cosmic potential. Never will they know until they come to recognize the One aspect of their reality they can never escape – that there is but One alternative…

One alternative, a simple choice hiding in the plain sight of today's cool breeze; what has come must also go. And in the ocean of consciousness that is humanity, the tides of man's affairs rise and fall with a moment's choice.

Within the simplest harmony of nature's tender song, there is but One truth – the truth of One. And with a narrow-minded perspective in a world where the dual nature of things seems to reign in a supremely misaligned fashion, a human who acts not to know the High Self does not truly act.

Trapped in the illusion of the Mighty Magician's magical mirage. Lured into the dungeon of self-decadence. Intoxicated by the grandness of one's own hypothetical self.

Forever will the trap remain as long as the giving away of the true essence of the One's greatest gift to humanity – Vision – continues to be dealt into the hand of the Maleficent Magician.

The Maleficent Magician seeks to mystify the mind of the one who chooses to remain in the mists of illusion – the false reality brought about by the story told from the mouth of perception.

—

"When," the Oracle asked, "when will you see beyond that which you already know does not matter?"

"Does not matter?" the child replied, obviously not understanding her.

"You are earnest in your desire to know," the Oracle said, "that much is obvious. Yet you cannot see beyond that which you already know does not truly matter."

"Why?" the child asked

"Only you can answer that question, for only you can know the reason you make the choices you do. But then again, what is a choice if all You *see* is pain and suffering?"

"So you're saying I do this to myself?"

"Is that what I'm saying? You forget, it is not me saying these words to you, it is you, I merely give voice to what you already know; *I am the voice within* you that you have chosen to not listen to. What you see before you is only a projection of your own mind. It has nothing to do with me; *I merely recognize the you that you long to know but are afraid to embrace.*"

"If I already know this, then why am I here?" the child asked.

"Why are you here?" the Oracle turned and walked away...

# V<small>erse</small> 6

### Quantum Field Theory

**Quantum:** "Smallest quantity of energy; the smallest discrete quantity of a physical property such as electromagnetic radiation or angular momentum."[14]

**Field:** "Area of force; an area or region within which a force exerts an influence at every point."[15]

**Theory:** "Scientific principle to explain phenomena; a set of facts, propositions, or principles analyzed in their relation to one another and used, **especially** in science, to explain phenomena."[16] [emphasis added].

**Quantum Field Theory:** A theoretical framework for creating quantum mechanical models or systems. A quantum field is a quantum mechanical system containing a large, and possibly infinite, number of degrees of freedom.

—

[14] Encarta Dictionary: English (North America)

[15] Ibid.

[16] Ibid.

Wait… infinite number of degrees of freedom?

What is that supposed to mean?

A quantum field, i.e. Me, is a quantum mechanical system **possibly** containing an infinite number of degrees of freedom?

What does that mean?

A quantum field, the backdrop of that which is a quantity at *each point in the fabric of space-time.*

What is the essence of my quantum existence, apparently within an infinite number of degrees of freedom?

Can I deny the reality of my quantity within my quantum quality? Logically, can I deny the reality of my quantumness? My freedom?

# Segue 6

sit back… relax…

*said the sweet little humming bird*

no worries… no stress…

all the lies in your life

is just a myth,

there's nothing gone amiss…

*whispered the sweet little humming bird*


*Live* LIFE to live life,

the darkness inside

is the shell of hell

that must die

for the Tree of Life of

~I~

to exist on High!

*sang the sweet little humming bird*


no troubles

can exist

with the choice

to exist from within

the Existence of your Lifely existence,

the troubles bred

upon the men and women of earth

exist from the vision of a devilish existence

emanating from within the indecision of who "I" is?

…then the blame

…the shame

…that guilt playin game

it takes the name of "who I am."

*the little humming bird sang*

My Will creates the Reality of My existence

… My divine existence

… everliving kindness,

the sweetness

of purity

cannot be duplicated,

never truncated,

always underestimated from

within the bliss of ignorance.

Arise from the myth

of ignorance

to realize

the wise

sight

of

YOUR

LIFE*long*

ever*living*

divine Existence

in the highest Unity of Purity!


… … in the moments 'i' tries,

the moments 'i' cries with dry eyes

'i' swallows the pain and suffering,

'i' can't stand the pangs of suffering,

the pangs of "my" devilish existence,

the conflict bred from "my" decisions

becomes the psuedo-reality of "my" existence,

*sang the sweet little humming bird*

the Reality! 'i' seek(s) to see

sources eternally within

the deepest, most

secret sacred walls of the

divine heart,

given to all,

from Thee All's tender loving heart

the sweet *humming* bird *sang*

the humming bird sang...

the *sweet* humming bird *sang*

# V erse 7

## Quantum Electrodynamics

**Quantum:** "smallest unit used to measure a physical property."[17]

**Electrodynamics:** "Electricity's interaction with mechanical forces; a branch of physics that studies _how_ electric currents interact with magnetic and mechanical forces."[18] [emphasis added]

**Quantum Electrodynamics (QED):** A quantum field theory that describes the properties of electromagnetic radiation and its interaction with electrically charged particles. QED describes electrically charged particles (and their antiparticles) interacting with each other by the exchange of photons (packets of light).[19]

—

[17] Encarta Dictionary: English (North America)

[18] Ibid.

[19] Ibid.

The electromagnetic spectrum that contains all forms of identifiable light radiation has a tiny portion that is visible to the human eye. Beyond that which is visible to the naked eye exists the reality of all quantum fields interacting through the entire spectrum – electro-*dynamics*.

Within the interaction of all the particles of existence, the exchange of light from one entity to another defines the process through which *Life* propagates.

The exchange of light energy, from one entity or object to another, connecting one entity to another in the inherently relative entangled state of the fabric of space-time; the exchange is the dynamic of life.

The exchange is the dynamic of life…

The *exchange is* the *dynamic* of Life…

**What do you *choose* to exchange?**

# $S$egue 7

What is it that I see, in my mind, as the reality of, well, Reality?

Can a mind constrained by the limitations inherent in the relativistic nature of the frame of reference through which the mind perceives ever truly *know* anything about that which is beyond the frame?

Even that which is within the frame? All dynamics, principles and laws that regulate the existence of the frame are beyond the surface of the *appearances* of the frame. What something *appears to be on the surface*, is a preliminary *observation* of events playing themselves out according to the *basic way in which the fabric functions.*

So, what am I looking at?

Can I, in a limited state of reference, i.e. human intellect, ever understand that which is infinite and without any finite limits? Can I ever understand the timeless simultaneous potential that gives rise the perception of time and "reality?"

But first...

What's in a word?

Seriously, as you read these words, as these words move through your *conscious* awareness, what is "it" they represent?

Words are composed of letters. Sentences are composed of words. This is something well known to any literate Being. But what is it about the words that make them so powerful?

Ever heard the phrase, "the pen is mightier than the sword?"

If that statement is *true*, what makes it so?

Words are merely representations. Words cannot contain the actuality of that which they represent. Just as the President of the United States is merely a representative of the people who truly hold the power. The President is NOT an *equal exchange* for that which he/she represents. The President merely represents.

Just the same, words only represent that which truly holds the power. Infinite Truth. Truth beyond limitation, cannot be contained by something that is inherently limited, as is the case with words.

Words are in-form-ation, they are *in-form*. Along with that *form* also comes the inherent constraints that add to the mis-interpretation of that which the word represents.

If *all* words are representations, what is it that they represent?

Thus far it has been said words represent *that* which truly holds the power. What is *That*?

Interestingly enough, *"That"* is what philosophers, scientists and normal people in general have been curious to understand since there was a capacity to understand.

Funny thing is, the dynamics through which *That* interacts with *That* are what guide everyday life. These *guiding dynamics* could also be called "Laws," for lack of a more appropriate *word*.

A question to ask yourself is, "will I choose to be guided by these 'Laws,' or will I continue to think they don't pertain to me?"

Don't be fooled, *if* you find yourself in conflict,

**any** type of conflict, *then* in some way

you believe they don't pertain to you.

It is simply a matter of embracing that which *is*;

nothing more, nothing less…

the conflict fades in the moment of Now[20]

[20] Michael Phoenix

*~ breathing ~*

## Other Titles by Michael Phoenix

Visit https://MichaelPhoenix.me for more.
- "Of the First Magnitude" series
  - o Facing Revelation: An Emerging
  - o iRise: An Algorhythm of Freedom
  - o Algorhythmic Insight: Poetic Analysis of the Journey
- Body Integration & the One Minute Workout: Learning to Love the Body You're In
- On Eros
  - o Consensio
  - o Sensualitas
  - o Sublimatio

# Of The First Magnitude

## ~I~

### ~Volume 1~
## Facing Revelation
*An Emerging*

### ~Volume 2~
## iRise
*An Algorhythm of Freedom*

### ~Volume 3~
## Quantum Engineering
*Introspecting the Rabbit Hole*

### ~Volume 4~
## Algorhythmic Insight
*Poetic Analysis of the Journey*

www.ingramcontent.com/pod-product-compliance
Lightning Source LLC
Chambersburg PA
CBHW051739040426
42447CB00008B/1215